SELECTED POEMS

ROBERT MINHINNICK

SELECTED POEMS

CARCANET

This selection first published in 1999 by
Carcanet Press Limited
4th Floor, Conavon Court
12-16 Blackfriars Street
Manchester M3 5BQ

A CIP catalogue record for this book
is available from the British Library
ISBN 1 85754 383 1

The publisher acknowledges financial assistance
from the Arts Council of England

Set in 10pt Times by Bryan Williamson, Frome
Printed and bound in England by SRP Ltd, Exeter

Contents

from
A Thread in the Maze
(1978)

Old Ships

Old ships lie out in rust-coloured lagoons
Between the tide and marram-matted shore.
I watch the gulls gleam on the barbican
Of their stripped decks, the broken line of hulls.

Below me in the littered dunes
Are men attacking wreckage
With cutting-gear of blue steel.
From dawn I watch this toiling group

In huge gauntlets that grasp
The flame's snake head, and vizors
Where their eyes swim huge and white.
All day their oxy rages

Through this decrepit navy
Of coaster, frigate, submarine;
A squadron that plied
From mammary Glamorgan

To the stamp-album countries,
The Gold-Coast, Nicaragua,
Or made Atlantic war.
In final dock each vessel

Is deftly disembowelled,
Their rudimentary structures
Like the skeletons of dinosaurs,
(Those easels of bone

Groaning on huge hinges,)
The hulkings utterly destroyed.
And scrap-men appear, like the Fury family,
Red-haired, hard-skinned, articulate,

The knives of their Irish whittling bargains
I, paying cash, have to resist.
But behind, respectably mackintoshed,
Hair thinning, step the retired sailors

Come to look. I watch them from
My sea-cabin, their slow and puzzled progress
Round the hulks, the beach a grey field
Quilted with burnt upholstering.

Brazen or bewildered they return,
The questions always achingly unasked:
Where are they now, the cables, chains and spars,
The long investments of their lives

In these smashed ships?
But the loco-men, the fire-eaters,
Brilliant lances melting through the plates,
See only ferrous detritus

And ganglions of steel they must burn off
Before the winter light dies on the sea,
And these old ships, so slowly overwhelmed,
Submerge and move beyond recovery.

Salvage

Children of ten or twelve
Transfer a traditional skill with horses
To ancient lorries and cars. They go jousting
Over the Tremorfa moorland, loud with the privileges
Of their raggedness

And illiteracy.
Hidden in a smashed martello, out of range
Of the gaffer's cuff and loud harangue, they watch men
    Salvaging the hulk of 'The Flying Fox',
        A rusted naval craft

    Gutted from deck to brine
Filled bilge, – while faint on the wind come sounds
Of the remote city, the retreating tide,
    As the Channel shifts its immense cold acre
        A little farther from

    The shore, revealing a
Tundra streamered with weed, an obscene
Exposure of a city's sludge. Walking out of a job,
    I end exile in a landscape of exhaustion:
        And am happy to retreat,

    But the hammering on
The iron hull, the hoarse windward singing
Of sea-carrion travel with me down a coast poisoned
    By people, crossboned with shipwreck. And there is
        No shaking off one's own defeat.

A Profile in Iron

Ganging the men, he warms himself
At the furnace of their breath.
Cynically, they eye his youth, holding
Their knuckles against frost's white razors,
Before demurring, finally setting to.

Turned twenty now with wife and infant son,
Already second foreman in the yard,
Paul moves through the swarf with slovenly grace
Or stands surveying a stark inheritance.
Flicking an eye over the electric shears –

Poised like a vulture on a carcass of rust –
He interprets for me the thick Irish
Of the tatter-men, their larded hair
Bluer than jackdaw wings, as they drive
Through a landscape he has sculpted from steel.

Later, in the washroom, he is moved to speak.
I see his narrow profile, the skin
Drawn smooth as paper on his jaw,
The sour-milk complexion of winter,
And listen to the hard, clean syllable

Of the sexual act punctuate his drift
Of careful words as another man might
Inhale a cigarette. A single sucked breath
That fascinates with its regularity.
To each fierce platitude I respond:

Our hands are bright with the green paste
Meant to dissolve oil. Anointed thus,
We may approach each other formally,
Two strangers who have found themselves
Suddenly vulnerable. We share

This experience through the hot water,
Our words clinging to air like steam's grey net,
Knowing outside lies the safety of routine
Where our smiles will slew if eyes collide,
But only for the sake of ritual.

In the south, adding clangour to the sea's
Deep bass has spread an iron field.
I watch Paul slowly pick his way
Through that man-scavenged territory,
Establishing a claim with his eyes.

Loud gulls rise up on wide hinged feet,
The filth floats on the narrow sea,
But one remains behind while we depart:
A boy who chains the gate against the night,
Makes fast the ingots of his chosen trade:
Who flourishes where I feel myself fail.

Sap

Where the stream ox-bowed
And we stood on a bulwark
Of planks and turf, the current
Made its darkest passage,
A black stillwater, treacherous
Beneath a sheen of scum.

Once, and once only, a trout rose,
Its lean sides gleaming like
A knife between the stones,
Crimson shadow at its belly.
Yet how often was the only sound
Not the Ffornwg or our
White thrash after fish,
But the thinnest flute of the sap
Maintaining its single note
A long minute in my head
As I imagined that pressure
Of water rising through the trees,
Streams moving vertically
And spilling in a silent turbulence
Along the boughs, a river

Flowing there beneath the bark,
The sap, singing, even as flesh
Leaned white and stunned
Against the visible current,
And the gwrachen like a small
Green stick swam past the hand.

Eels at Night

Finely poised above the crawling Ffornwg
I watch the strange night turbulence of eels,
For eels like sperm thick spawn the river vat,
Inscribing circles on tar-black water,
Their strings of flesh a skein that instinct ties.

The terror of eels is their writhing fleece,
The corpse that Ffornwg shreds with slow razors.
Into my own shadow I can plunge my hand
And feel the slippery texture of congealing eels
Like a wound opened in myself, our common skin.

Get an eel in the fist they say, and that's money,
But the cold coin that I grasp now surely buys
More than is guessable, but something like knowledge
Of a life joined with mine, gnashing in blood's long pod,
And a joint affirmation of the hollow flesh.

Dragonfly

Bullet of stained glass glancing out of the traffic.
Some trembling cellophane I find at my feet.
Handspan of colours; daubs from the palette of light.
Black honeycomb pattern embroidered on wings.
Carnage in October: blue scalds of the dusk.
Somnolent. Extinguished. Jewel of pus on dragonfly snout.
I hold in my hand a crucifix on the Cribwr road.

Bryony

Against the military thorn
Its berries hold a tropic promise –
The colours of temptation
And the poison bottle.

On vines of white hay
I have felt the vitriol
Hardening beneath the berry skins,
Imagined the thick sap curdling

Like the embryos of thrushes,
Cold eggs I blew to new brightness.
Now breaking the cable of bryony
For a handful of the polished grapes

I find a rash of tough carbuncles
Brilliant with pus, as all around
Poison ferments in yellow wickerwork
Of straw, a lattice on the hedge's ribs.

And shocking, this abundance of bryony,
Like discovering the body
Of some richly-decayed creature,
A reminder that the world

Looms huge with threat, can overpower
With thin secretion of its fruit,
Or this knot that whitest bryony ties
Around a life with its tight string.

Ivy

The parasite itself a tree
Upon a tree; dense mirrored leaves
And berries' soft eruptions
Releasing their odour of childhood.

This ivy world engulfed me as a boy,
Its dark tunnels an orient
Of summer pungencies, filled with
Dry and choking dandruff of the vines.

Its trunks like human fists would grasp
And suffocate oak or sycamore
In wrestlers' holds, grow grey and muscular
As rope, strangling, intractable.

For hours in a garden's undergrowth
I sat invisible, content to breathe
Its stagnant air, thick and heavy, potent with
The sharp aroma of the rogue ivy,

The smell alive, a vivid taint
That suddenly disturbs a mind
Untroubled by its force for half a life.
World into world: I am brought down

To childhood, or raised up again
To meet that private person I once was:
A boy who closed the branches on the sky,
Knew ivy's acid fragrance on his skin.

Short Wave

I try to tune in, but Europe's blurred voice
Becomes stranger with the movement of the dial.

All stations seem to give a fragment of
Performance, – Mozart disarmed by a fizzled
Prodigy; innumerable cliques of wordsmiths.

As the electric crackles I make believe
I am composing an avant-garde symphony,
A sound poem for a hall of idiot speech.

But behind the static are moments of sanity:
A string quartet and interesting chanteuse,
Then histrionics at a play's climax.

For some reason, a hubbub of languages
And dim music becomes more important
Than any scheduled programme. It suits

My mood perhaps, this indecipherable mayhem
Of newscasters and sopranos, and the long
Returns to electronic gibbering.

Somewhere, behind a rockband's sudden squall,
A morse message is tapped out. For a few seconds
It is clear, articulate, before melting

Into Europe's verbiage. It was not mayday.
And I twist the dial a hairsbreadth into jazz.

19

The Night Switchboard

The switchboard is a deck of light above
The town. One floor with a rubber plant,
A security guard, and angles of glass

Whose white clocks spin in a monotone.
Up there the silence is solid with its
Own odour; the smell of new plastics,

Emulsion, the chrome and foam-backed furniture.
But with your head wired to every kiosk
And bar, the voices come lisping across

The distances, asking for taxis, the police,
Or merely the rigmarole of words.
4 a.m. The hour of silence. An

Occasional gasp for emergency services.
But make a connection and you greet
The noise. Tiny metallic voices crawling

Over each other like bees in a black
Chamber, a swarm that disintegrates
Inside your head, becomes a vital

Current, ceaseless, eager, insistent as
Electricity. So you listen until
The town wakes, when the cold coin drops through

A quandary of light. And it is a
Relief to greet the morning shift with the
First brazen words of the day. To change

Chairs and responsibilities, go out
Into the cool, dark air, see the switchboard
Like a tier of light above the street.

Weapons for Survival:
in Liverpool Cathedral

You talked about a girl from Sligo
Who kept a house in Barry Street,
Then directed me through city rain
To a place where I could sleep.

And tonight, with the gale slackening,
I wonder where you find yourself:
Again perhaps in the cathedral's
Cool sanctuary, under that fat spire,

The roof of painted glass where we met
And listened to a distant congregation,
The words of an English mass tolling
Like water through enormous silence.

But far below that whispered flood
You kept a keener vigil. I watched you dive
To the floor and extract the dirty stubs
From a Players' pack a man had left behind,

Some new additions to the day's small change.
And I remember I could see your belly
Grey and bulbous straining at your shirt,
The plastic sport-shoes with the broken seams.

And I knew there was something I had to ask,
Like where you travelled, how you found your food,
Waiting for the word that would define the man,
Listening, in fact, for a hard luck tale

That never came. For when our eyes met
It was mine that slid away, down the dark
Transept of that echoing church
To a brilliant annexe where a man poured wine.

1921: The Grandfather's Story

1976. Europe uniquely dry,
A vast blond savanna;
No end to such weather.
But the grandfather's tale
Concerned another year,
A striking, starved Glamorgan
The continent of his experience.

Ffornwg reduced to one
Green rope of water, glutinous
With gnats, and the village men
Moithered by heat, the latest scabs,
And an army of imported police
Billeted like Stuart troops.

Moonlight over a deserted
Countryside. Only the birds
Audible in air tarnished
By water's slow decay.
Boys scrabbling for coal-crumbs
In the forbidden pits. No rain three months.
Even Nant Iechyd rusty, dangerous.

But what he recalls tonight,
The grandfather amongst the bar's
Shirtsleeved crush, are the
Extraordinary voices of dying trout,
Like the mewling of newborn kittens,
Their shrill tumult shocking his mind
As he ladled fish from a shrinking pool,
Twenty-two thin and mottled bodies
Like half-opened jack-knives in the dry grass,
And only the eels, a villainous
Purple escaping, and the bells
Striking four as he walked home,
And the sun rising.

Oxford

Travelling, we exchanged first words.
You read a letter and we gazed across
   The vast gunmetal lake that had drowned Oxfordshire,
   The flood grown rusty in the late sun.

And your eyes became brilliant in the smoke of your face
When you talked of your children, writing carefully
   For me their strong English names,
   And the name of your lover beneath.

And later, walking the city, looking for rooms,
I began to think that here was a familiar, adrift for an hour
   Or a day like myself, simply moving
   Amongst the supermarkets and immaculate quads,

Two strangers revealing themselves
In the winter evening's vitriolic gloom,
   Discovering each other, sharing that sacrament
   Of the conjunction of lives that comes once.

But returning Jane, I must fix my gaze
On this glittering fen, smoking as it drains away,
   Uncovering the lowland, a colour of banknotes,
   Like the undramatic contours of a life.

Chance, all that banal circumstance
Of meeting, knowing, casual farewell, becomes now
   Dangerously imbued with words.
   Already I have imprisoned you

Within the poem's lie, your eyes
The glass of metaphor, the flesh that I could not deceive
   The texture of this page. How eagerly I would betray
   You, stranger, for the telling, cruel word.
      Since I cannot reach you any other way.

from
Native Ground
(1979)

Images from Tremorfa

The incense of a tall brazier
Like bitter odour of burnt horn
A hot acridity inside my head.

I slide off early over cushioned mud,
Passing East Moors, a blitzed town
Burning and deserted, fire's

Intricate horizon a yellow
Thread woven into the dark.
Moving alone on the grey sea-moor

After today's clerking of the ferrous trade
I remember the Greek in the precious-
Metal shop; Mr Stassinopolos,

His sweat a helmet of new steel
Tight across his brow, and the Furys'
Camp, caravans beneath the iron scree,

Dogs loping behind child acrobats.
Cold, cold with a vengeance now,
The winter light solidified, opaque.

For the last time I move through Queen's Wharves
And watch the derelicts, the fuse
Burning in their eyes; like terrorists

Carefully carrying the gelignite
Of their experience towards the town's bright glass.
Tonight, I share their cause, its sure defeat.

Grandfather in the Garden

Digging was always my worst work.
After ten minutes I would blow
My scalding hands and watch him fork
Quite effortlessly the rain-heavy clay
Of a new garden, meticulous and slow
Labour that soon tired a boy.

All his life a cultivator
Of the soil's best things, ingenious
Exterminator of what opposed his sure
Design. Summers wet or dry found him
Aware of deep conspiracies of earth
To damage or destroy the year's triumph.

Thus he squared his jaw, donned ancient
Clothes, and set to digging out his
Fears. Late evenings I'd be sent
To call him in, a dark and elemental
Shape by then, the ruins of a young man's face
Still visible behind the years, the toil.

A labourer and architect,
He taught patience in slow lessons
And one man's dedication to a craft.
From his cracked hands I watched the brittle seed
Cast surely for the future, the unborn;
Those acts of affirmation his deep need.

Drinks after the Funeral

Now grandfather in your black suit
With drinks after the funeral,
Gently curling a forefinger
Purple with gout around the handle

Of a pint glass, it's time to reminisce,
The past being a territory
You own more of than most. Survivor!
What glows in you today

Is not the fire of alcohol,
A furnace stoked for sixty years,
Still blazing. Raising your tone,
White shaven head thrown back in bull's laughter,

The spittle of your politics
Flies free, a special sour phlegm
Reserved for Tories and the Nationalists,
Those two distinctive enemies

In your black and white world.
The narrow, deep alignments still exist,
The struggle never ending
As you toss an old protagonist

On the tusks of argument.
Old boar at bay of course you guess
The nets are closer now. In church
Your voice was a cracked bell

Tolling for the vanished years,
Slowly growing hoarse and faltering.
So come, let's drink a toast to your new world
Remembering its first principle:
To keep a generous measure in each glass.

On a Portrait of John Dee
(Spy, Astrologer, Mathematician)

This black canvas an Elizabethan night.
Only the dimmed lantern of the face,
That hand holding a testament
Obstruct the gloom. Appropriate

The artist's doubt. How to decipher
The code of this man's life, the lean
Courtier, bittern-necked, in corset of stiff lace,
His slightest thread of smile itself

A wordless cryptogram? Cold oils preserve
A pale astrologer whose superstitious
Scholarship transferred the evening's bestiary
Of stars to royal horoscopes, whose harmless

Chess became a skill deployed round living kings.
Such brilliant paradox must fascinate.
This squalid agent of a vicious state
Grew older, found retirement, and poses here

Respectable and rich. Profound John Dee
Your life suggests the real, essential irony
Our flatter lives conceal. You, modernist,
A riddle to our reasoning, our mediæval mind.

Dorothy

Outside on the mountain road
The beggars look over the wall,
Two ruined soldiers holding
Their rags of uniform against
Another spring spate, whipped
English conscripts eating your bread.

A headache again, and a thrush
Singing at the beck in the orchard.
Two geese unplucked in the kitchen.
Today, as always, you scrawled
Your few lines into the book,
Quietly, quietly, each entry

A fact, a precise statement
Of observation and accomplishment.
The day so long. You filled it
With baking, a bone-chilling walk
As far as the pike. A letter came,
And some beggars who are still there

Squatting in the wet grass, two
Gangling men as tall as muskets,
The tails of their greatcoats fluttering.
So dark for May, you cannot read.
In the stone room the small flowers
Called stitchwort, white as shirtbuttons,

Are starting to die. When the moon
Shines you can see the lake
Through the window gleaming like lead.
There is a man's voice in the bedroom,
Half-word, half-cough. A cry in a fever.
You get up and go to him.

J.P.

Trespassing, we were caught like moths
In the headlight trap of the Wolseley.
We glimpsed his face behind the windscreen,
The bright figurine on the car-bonnet

Pointing at our guilt. In that world
He was legend, a tiny octogenarian
In panama and summer suit
Poised with secateurs above a rose-stem,

Or tapping with the polished ferrule
Of his cane through the gutter dust.
I remember the inquisitive gleam
Of his eyes, head cocked like a woodmouse,

As he regarded the extent of our crime,
Still the magistrate at the bench,
The jealous landowner. In the mansion-house
We had burgled rooms he never opened,

Broken the seal of the dust. And now,
Awaiting sentence, we shifted resentfully
In that hot stain of light. For Llangewydd's
Square mile of history, its cwms and

Slow decaying farms, the blaze of lawn about
The magistrate's estate, was an inheritance
We claimed. Even then the idea was alive
Within us: we belonged; we continued;

For ours was an instinct that mastered fear
And fired a tribal defiance of that
Black car as we stood our ground,
Staring together into its powerful beam.

Peregrine R.I.P.

Without a woman you were doomed
   And whisky is the worst wife.
Slowly you learned the futility
Of trying and accepted the dereliction
   Of those burnished afternoons
When the farm trembled like a mirage

About you, horseflies sawing over
   The dung, a brazier of ragwort
In every crack of the *beili*. And lying
In the rick with a cider bottle
   You could afford to damn the lot
Of us, our compassion's small change

The price of a drink. Thomas Peregrine:
   The name has a pedigree
You never inherited. Strong Englishry
Dwindled to your gentle bewilderment
   With a world that turned its back.
So you retreated, nursing your wound

In the kitchen, the skin under your
   Stubble ice-grey. I watched you
Crack the armour of ticks with a thumbnail
And fling the bodies in the grate.
   On the bars they flared
As brightly as match-heads. And that is

As close as I ever came, seeing you burst
   Fat ticks, an illumination
Of blood you never felt. In the end,
You said, we will all walk away
   From one another. But you
Were already gone, skidding down

   The track to the dirty manger
   And the uncomplaining company of beasts;
The quiet, private extinction we wished for you.

The Drinking Art

The altar of glasses behind the bar
Diminishes our talk. As if in church
The solitary men who come here
Slide to the edges of each black
Polished bench and stare at their hands.
   The landlord keeps his own counsel.

This window shows a rose and anchor
Like a sailor's tattoo embellished
In stained glass, allows only the vaguest
Illumination of floor and ceiling,
The tawny froth the pumps sometimes spew.
   And the silence settles. The silence settles

Like the yellow pinpoints of yeast
Falling through my beer, the bitter
That has built the redbrick
Into the faces of these few customers,
Lonely practitioners of the drinking art.
   Ashtrays, a slop-bucket, the fetid

Shed-urinal, all this I wondered at,
Running errands to the back-doors of pubs,
Woodbines and empty bottles in my hands.
Never become a drinking-man, my
Grandmother warned, remembering Merthyr
   And the Spanish foundrymen

Puking their guts up in the dirt streets,
The Irish running from the furnaces
To crowd their paymaster into a tavern,
Leather bags of sovereigns bouncing on his thigh.
But it is calmer here, more subtly dangerous.
   This afternoon is a suspension of life

I learn to enjoy. But now
The towel goes over the taps and I feel
The dregs in my throat. A truce has ended
And the clocks start again. Sunlight
Leaps out of the street. In his shrine of glass
    The landlord is wringing our lives dry.

The House

I lie across the rafters of the loft
Holding the torch. From the junction box
Wires twist into darkness, a crumbling
Skein of red and black under sackcloth
Of webs. For three stifling hours

In the attic's heat I have cursed
This challenge, frustrated by
Electricity – the merciless current
That will not come. And the silence
Of the house offers no clue. Matching

Myself against its fifty years,
The solid rooms and gables of this redbrick
Terrace, I must establish my own
Permanence. For territory is not
Bought or sold but fought over: it is

The first instinct, the small, unremarkable
Warfare of our lives. Yet crouched in this
Hot attic room my sweat has turned to ice.
The torchbeam's yellow cylinder
Identifies the dust, shapes from life

That have served their time and been abandoned
By the house. And I stare, fascinated,
At the dead. The faces of those who once called
This house home. Like them, like this frail
Blade of light, the house has swallowed me.

The Children

Their squints and stammers disappeared,
The crooked teeth straightened somehow.
Difficult to tell if they need you now,
These fastidious young, your children,
Sipping glittering gin through their own ice.

Talk of experience, you're still the novice:
Already they have covered the world,
England, France, it's a motorway ride
In a friend's car, the music blasting
As they overtake your careful saloon.

Yet you still pretend to know these strangers,
Passing round photographs of children
They used to be, the horses ridden,
The mountains climbed. Look closer, you think,
And you will see yourself, a figure

In the background smiling at something
Out of the picture. Yet you will wonder
At your own permanence. Make supper then,
You're good at that, but already
They are waving goodbye through the frozen

Brilliance of windscreens, driving
To a life where their backs form a tight
Circle. Are you ever discussed?
There's never a silence in their intricate conversations;
And they forgot to mention when they are coming again.

Hide and Seek

The damp mahogany shade
Between chapel and the terraces
    Concealed a territory
I thought only we children knew.

Bindweed spread its bitter
White rosettes over headstones, the dew
    Gleamed like porcelain in the stillness
As I listened for my friends to come

And find that hiding-place –
Under the hogweed where the graves
    Were thrown open like drawers
And snails unwound their silver

On my jersey; under the hogweed
With the dead in their dormitory.
    But awaiting a crackle of voices
I knew even then it would not be

Friends that found me out,
Or set me running from that
    Startling intimacy, the yellow
Stitched cranium, the opening pit.

Native Ground

In my grandparents' home the weekly treat
   Was the hard globe of a pomegranate.
With the juice on my chin I would watch
   The woman rinsing pans, scabs on her
Knuckles and the fat yellow wedding-ring

Gleaming in dishwater. Every day
   Of her life she would submerge with those pots,
Throwing the gossip over her shoulder
   In an ugly jewellery of words
I had not learned to value. What was she

Talking about all the time? The names
   And the proverbs were strange as the rind
Of the pomegranate, that difficult fruit.
   So I fumbled with its scarlet honeycomb
And stared through the window at my grandfather,

Bent it seemed permanently towards the earth,
   Always the man apart, but scrabbling now
With the creeping flower called pimpernel
   Scattered everywhere like confetti.
And then I would turn and yawn and listen;

And listen, pinpricking the jewels
   Of the pomegranate, not wondering about
History, that tangible subject I might love.
   There and then I was happy, if bored.
And time added another piece to the mosaic.

In Class

I try my best but the word won't come;
I acknowledge that my speech is lame;
I am the child with the burnt tongue.

Christ, it hammers at my skull,
This sound that I cannot expel,
It grows until it seems to fill

All consciousness. One frail word
A trap only silence can avoid.
While others read

I sweat
Listening to my blood's journey,
The thin blue pulse that throbs above the eye.

But when I scream
The hated school hangs breathless
About me. Boys' blunt faces
Like the pebbles they put into my mouth.

The Gamekeeper

I feared his stoop and hollow face,
An accent that was rural Gloucestershire.
And now I wonder if we met today
Would I turn and run as I ran
In childhood from him, leaving my name
Slashed white in bark for the English gamekeeper.

These days I walk the same estate
Looting its creamy elderflower,
Pushing hip-deep through fern to secret
Enclosures, but often I think
Of the excitement I felt, hearing
His dogs unleashed in full-throated

Pursuit of our fleeing gang, their
Copper pelts plastered with stinging
Brookwater. That old man died and I
Grew up, and trespassing is not the same
Without his narrow shadow stooping
Over me, his tweeds the colour of beechshade

The perfect camouflage. I miss
The danger, the fright as hot as
Nettlerash on a boy turning with
Broken breath to the dancing retrievers
And hearing the other side of the wood
The tired prosecution of his name.

After a Friendship

Still clear, that morning his family moved,
The lorry carrying furniture and people
Towards Swansea. I never waved
But breathed at the window the sweet-stale

Air of the empty house. And walked home.
If there was grief I have forgotten it,
But from then on things were not the same.
Grammar-school, homework, rugby-kit

Filled my time. I learned to become
Invisible and wrote the days' timetable
In an exercise book. My uniform
Had a heart-shaped badge and its black wool

Steamed in the rain. We were all proud.
And seven years passed like the days'
Seven lessons and he slowly dwindled
From my mind, a small ghost who preys

Now suddenly but for good reason
On imagination and memory.
It was never repeated, that season
Of friendship: a ten-year-old boy

With mad eyes, a truant, a sleeper-out
In haystacks brought down his fist
With a cobble in it and a gout
Of blood fell like a grape into the dust.

Fear and learning; deliberate
Childish violence. Like steel and flint
We sparked each other to the great
Discovery of ourselves. And went

Our ways. Children with their tough minds
Would understand. Seeing my blood
Did not scare us. It ran for the parting of friends.
We both knew we were going away for good.

Rhigos

The cannon-smoke rolling
Off the Beacons engulfs the car.
The violence is over
Yet a promise of lightning
With its cordite tang hangs over
The khaki drab of Hirwaun.

41

Above this mist they gaze
From the stacked flats:
Faces between the turrets,
Hands clenched without weapons.
The only armour here
Is isolation that toughens

The mind, hardens eyes
That stare from siege. I think
Of the people who live
On these battlements: old
Women white and frail as moths,
The men mulattoed by alcohol,

Their frustration which burnt
A hole in life itself burnt out.
Leaving nothing. And as we grind
Over the mountain gridiron
I know they are seeking us
And our movement's illusion

Of freedom, those old people
Standing at their balconies
In the fresh wind, yet
Seeing instead this prow
Of Glamorgan – the black
And naked Rhigos, a whalebacked

Massif that supports
Nothing of their life, that
Is no comfort, yet is the earth
To which they are fused –
Its cloud and violet skeins of light;
An unendurable rock.

Atlases

Gear-teeth snag, another reckless change.
The engine labours on this gradient
But all at once we are high and over,
Definitely arrived. Summer half-spent
Has ripened the still air; something
Familiar here, something inexplicably
Foreign merging like light and shadow,
Making me sad for what I might reject:
Square farmhouses of barley-coloured stone
Set amidst paddocks where horses graze,
Tall hunters with their fetlocks black with dew,
Existences ringed round by silence, a haze
Of flies, horse-stench, fields of green savoys
And fields of grain, then woods and coombs,
A pool with lilies and the dark, erratic
Tench a voice disturbs. I think of rooms
Where heads of teenage boys bend to atlases,
And the English counties, each a different
Watercolour, fill the maps. Fishing,
Farming, the aggressive verbs of industry
Meaninglessly described. And yet, an
Idea of England is salvaged from the page,
A comforting, unspoken prejudice
Learned and forgotten at that resentful age
Returning now quick and alarmingly
As I slow at a signpost and barleystraw
Swirls in the exhaust. This is the place
Where I could be myself, the country that I
Loved from atlases. So I stare through dusk
At the blurred surface of things, change gear,
Wipe the window of a stain of insect-blood,
And leave behind what's still not understood.

from
Life Sentences
(1983)

China 1830

Across the hillside comes a line of men:
Dawn's extraordinary light like the cholera
Party moving through China, whitelime on the skin
Turning to ash in the dew of flickering Merthyr.

In the taverns the burnt men show their scars;
Lacerations of fire where the furnace spat.
It's bandit country that lives by its own law,
That snoring ale-stained giant its emperor.

And flourishing in Dowlais now the dialect
Of iron is more powerful than psalms;
The vocabulary of the engineer, industry's elect,
Has drawn the populations from the quiet farms,

Coal-hewers, turners, every creed and sect
Sleeping shoulder to shoulder on the tavern boards,
While the English language ravenous for words
Goes swaggering like a drunkard on the street.

from *The Death of Johnny Owen*

A year later I think of how you died,
Forgetting where and why and most of all
The name of your executioner,
That hard, simple man they cheered from the ring,
Head bowed, sweat-brightened, face cowled like a monk.

China : a district of Merthyr Tydfil in the early 1800s.

47

What's clearest is the video's imagery
Of a pale cadaver ready for the morgue,
Your brain reduced to one thin brilliant line
On the scanner in the graph of extinction.
A life switched off like a television set.

No boxing man, I queued for newspapers,
Let the ink stain my hands as the headlines
Hailed a martyrdom, and in blurred profile
You posed again for combat and brief celebrity,
A cartoon face shadowed by naked fists.

Our comfort is the deaths you have escaped:
Erskine's devastated speech, slurred words
Thrown like a drunk's punches, the Louis wheelchair
Parked at every championship ringside,
All broken gods and secretly despised.

Thirty Years Later the Drunk Man Tells the Truth

Thirty years later the drunk man tells the truth.
How Albert Pierrepoint arrived with his travelling bag
And Matan was taken out of the condemned cell,
No collar or boots, his stubble rough as peppercorn;
A last erection, pathetic and involuntary,
But a prayer of his own like the priest's hushed rite.
Then the hatch dropped open and he stepped in the grave.

But it was wartime and better men had died.
V.E. Night and Montgomery smiling in the *News Chronicle*,
Alamein already part of English mythology
As a drunk man on the first of too many drunks,
The happy squaddie, rolls towards Cardiff gaol
And the hangman enters the turnstile, sniffing the drains
Of a bombed city, brushing the crease in his gaberdine.

Over the rim of your beer you explode this history.
Thirty years of scrabbling for the elusive quid,
Fraud and drunkenness and theft and prison slops;
But nothing as terrible as Matan's walk
Up a disinfected corridor, and Pierrepoint
In state's regalia waiting like a bridegroom
In the jamb. Two men who touched briefly and were gone.

And you have worn them like the Alamein ribbons,
The general's smile. For the horror and for the pride.
An innocent man was destroyed in Cardiff gaol –
Matan lying newly-stitched in the mortuary,
Pierrepoint hurrying to the station, clutching the half
Of his ticket. And you, released today, the drunken soldier,
Thirty years later the drunk man telling the truth.

Driving in Fog

Driving in fog I part the crowded air,
Then the night falls huge and white across the car.

It is as if I stopped believing in the world
The dark conceals, preferring the immense, cold

Flowerings of fog the headlights stain
To dull amber, the solderings of rain

That glisten on the crawling vehicle.
Yet I never seem to break its streaming wall,

Never reach that moment I can rightly say
Here it begins: always it remains a yard away

In the blurred crowding of fields that overhang
The road, the pale entangling yarns

Of my own breath. Here is not the rain's
Assault, the sullen-strange communion

Of the snow. This is no weather but the bland
Present's arrest, for even the trees stand

Like inked letters half-erased. All traffic
Stops. The fog's white sweat gives radiance to the dark.

In a shrunken world I wait for it to pass,
But the fog like countless faces crowds the glass.

Sunday Morning

I choose back lanes for the pace they will impose,
    An old perspective half forgotten
Surprising me now as the world slows
With these things the broad road lacked:
    Carboys of vitriol stacked in a garage,
Orange hooks of honeysuckle gripping a wall.

Here a church window becomes an arch of light
    And the pitching of a hymn a brief
Infusion of the air. Voices, and low
Indistinguishable words, the organ's bass
    The foundation for a ritual
I trespass in, that suddenly

Intensifies the day. On the other side
    I picture them: the ranked devout
Pulling the ribbons from the black prayerbooks
And each with his or her accustomed doubt
    Submitting to a poetry
Triumphant as the church's muscular brass.

Thus Sunday morning: a gleaning
  Of its strange wisdoms. The certainty
Of hymns comes with me through a different town
Of derelict courts and gardens, a stable
  Where a vizored man beats sparks from a wheel,
An old man splitting marble in a mason's yard,

The creamy splinters falling into my mind
  Like the heavy fragments of hymns,
Then walking on, much further, this morning being Sunday.

Catching My Breath

At midnight I walk over the bailey-bridge,
The mallows waving in dark plantations
Below me at the river's edge, the finest
Paring of the moon quite red above the town.
There's nothing I can say that's praise enough.

No feeling yet, but a new perspective.
I've spent all day in the labour-ward
Listening to the women endure a rhythm
Of pain and gas and pain, the sounds from
Their own throats desperate as the cries of the newborn.

For twelve hours then, a spectator
As astonished fathers trooped out of the theatre,
Square rugby players in knife-edge blazers,
A mechanic with a sparse teenage moustache.
And all had stood where I have done

Strapped into gown and mask, watching
The beating of two hearts pencilled on endless
Tickertape, observing a woman's fury and despair
With strange dispassion. She came with a cry,
The sudden child, her skin like grapeskin,

A blue colour, the head fist-sized and punching
At the air, the long birth cable trussing her
Like flex. Now from my place on the bridge
I see the river-shingle gleam under water;
There's no feeling yet; only a place where it will be.
I lean on the parapet to catch my breath.

The Aerial

It's a town house built between the wars
Surrounded by a plot of frozen earth.
We pay each month, at night I bolt the doors,
And if this job saves money it's worth

Challenging the nerve. Winter's first snow
Is on the hills, the sea furrowed like ploughland;
I start to hate the people who below
Pass unconcerned, not knowing that I stand

On yellow chimney-stacks blackened by smoke,
Engraved with names of potteries in Stoke-
On-Trent. How laughable, the things we come to know;
Poor steeplejack, I blink back vertigo

Until at last I'm taller than the house,
The aerial turning like a weathervane
In my hands, six feet of hollow steel aimed south
And east, seeking the invisible signal.

In a room below a screen has cleared;
The world hurls images we can't escape:
I'm overwhelmed by sudden freezing vision,
A man who climbs, a searching fragile shape.

The Boathouse

The sawyers lie outside the shed,
Its blades motionless for the first
Time today, the men silent, sprawled
On a floor of white dust, their
Haversacks before them, and behind,
The heaps of sawn wood, the logs stacked
Like new loaves, the smell as sweet.

In my mind they will sit there forever,
The village men in feudal grouping,
Craftsmen of the estate, and my mother
Saying 'Good morning sir' to the gentleman
As he passes, to the brassy heads
Of cartridges in his twill. A smile
For the girl remembered always.

It's finished now, the whole place
Closed down. Employment's found outside
The creamery, the vinery and grange
Farm that fed inherited wealth,
That tiny, epic world once sufficient
To itself, working perfectly and
Observed from the boathouse by this

Trespasser hidden amongst anglers'
Tackle, the moss-coloured lake sliding
Under the boards. Suddenly everyone
Had fallen asleep – nurserymen,
Chauffeurs, kitchenmaids – the hour
Went unstruck. There was nothing
But silence and the soft putrescence

Of the boathouse, the shoals of ochre mud
Where water stood. Through a rotten
Lath the lake slipped in. The vans arrived,
I heard the barking of the country
Auctioneers, 'Good morning sir
Sir sir' of my mother talking to the dead,
A population slamming doors on a way of life.

The Party

When a pig was killed everything was eaten;
Only the bristling hide dispensable,
And that was scalded and scraped off.
Pig-killing day meant a party in the village,
Cider and stone-ginger unstoppered
When the working ceased, the familiar
Talk of the slaughter-man wiping his
Blades on dockleaves, pig-blood dark as blackberries
Trodden into the dust. And then
A joke, or ritual, alarming to some:
The youngest child placed inside the split carcase,
And lifted out laughing from the wound's long slot.

The Brook

Infamous for eels, bearded, wrist-thick,
Some wound like electric cable round a gaff,
Their truncheon heads thrusting at the air.
How cold they were, vicious, familiar;
Generations coiled together on bright gravel.

But because they grew so great I'd devil
Myself to wade upstream, thinking of eels
Black and vulcanized like bicycle tyres
Knotting my legs, my drowned face with the eyes
Eaten. Tree roots waving in the current.

Then my mind was like the stream's ferment
Of lives, the water round the carcase of a steer
Disturbed by the invisible, the secretive
Come to feast. But if the brook was death's element,
The harmless eels were the evil I'd invent.

Burmese Tales

After the swim I move across a beach
Pale as stubble, seating underfoot.
Each wave I remember as a garment
Thrown aside, a chill skin of water
Stiffening into salt and cracked sunburn.

The small sand leeches cling against my legs,
Transparent bodies I watch slowly
Darken like mercury with the blood heat.
And I recall again at the same age
This was my father's daily occupation,

Washing the scum of mangrove-water
From his skin, applying with a surgeon's
Neutral skill, or holding Bogart-like
A cigarette to the feasting creatures,
The hot tobacco shrivelling fat leech-flesh.

His Burmese tales show lurching muleteers
Packing across a spine of hills,
The squads of dark, unmilitary Welsh
Arriving at a village strung
With the waxen rosaries of shrunken heads.

Some things there are to salvage from the waste.
History absorbs this too, and yet
It is his own perspiration I feel chafe
As he lifts the webbing on a green
Insect-thrumming dawn, sucks air. And endures.

And I could go on and on with him
Following the mules through the Shan states
Until the trees become China and the war ends.
His life my drama in the skull's arena,
But such imagery the one inheritance.

from
The Dinosaur Park
(1985)

The Dinosaur Park

Padlocked, green-white, the villas
Glint like bone in the dusk.
The road a dead-end but here's a path
Snaking between houses to a public
Garden. Its lawn's a rug of frost
Behind chainlink where crocuses
Have pushed through stems, white as
Cigarette-papers, the knifepoints
Of their colours: the cold meths-blue
Of steel, a fringe of darker blue.
The path moves on by turnstiles
And a locked kiosk, a bowls-sward
And the asphalt tennis courts.
It winds around the dinosaur park.

Off-season and it's shut. I bend a wire
And trespass over frost that shines
Like candlewax. Hummocks and trees,
And then the other trespassers,
Bolted on to sandy plinths,
Moored in the wrong time.
Out of the fantastic past they loom,
Great engines seized, the inert
Mechanics of some botched experiment.
Absurd, abject, the dinosaurs
Are the unimaginable fact.
I pace their world of huge pretence,
The museum quiet grown around the town.
And yet, what's real, as real as these
Vast creatures poised about the park?
The olive plastic of their skin
Under its icy lamination
Is dimpled like golfballs, their
Footprints shallow concrete moulds
Of birdbaths, ashtrays, litter-traps,
The eyeballs livid as traffic-lights.

History too must have its joke.
They're cartoons come to almost-life,
The dinosaurs, or might belong
To some children's crackling screen.
I've passed the park a score of times
But never glimpsed in its entanglement
These postures struck of combat,
Rage, the slow acknowledging of pain.
And strange to think such creatures shared
The common factors of our lives,
Hurt and hunger, fear of death,
The gradual discovery of betrayal.
But prey and predator are one
And are swallowed up by the omnivorous dark,
The watched, the watcher, and the mammoth's dazzling scythes.
Now level with the dinosaurs
The path runs on, there's no way back,
As shadows make their imperceptible surge.

The Saltings

1

The men in singlets, dark as Basques,
The women grizzled wands.

The grass is sparse, a few thistles
Where she sits down in front of the flats,

Fingering the globe of her belly,
The man's name needled on her arm.

2

When you are born dumb
There are only gestures to make.

Tattoos are badges of contempt,
A small defiance allowed here

Like the bottle smashed against the kerb,
The explosion of paint in the stairwell.

3

She is standing on the balcony
And her skin is white as heroin.

A child is pressed under her heart,
Curled up like a fossil there.

This is the life that persists beyond our thought
And has no one to speak for it.

The Coast

By single grains it slowly filled their lives.
Everything that stood against it
Was covered by the thin gold web of sand.

Under the door its drifting gauze, and through
The barley. Along shelves and into the privy
Rushed sand, ceaseless and mercurial.

A teeming of aphids over the leaves,
The passing of a whisper at the door
Was sand, building against useless iron.

Now out of the dune comes the remnant of that life.
A needle's eye packed with golden silt
And a polished edge of broken pottery.

Down a hundred feet, or one, the fields
Are ready for the plough. The plastics lie
Not quite as deep, are dimly mauve and cream

Like winter bulbs. Our ground is blurring,
Losing its angles, but the brand-names push
Out of the sand their familiar epitaphs,

And a shattered bottle reassures that our claim
Was made. Here a tidy rank of caravans
Floats axle-deep upon the creeping tide.

Surfers

September evenings they are here after work,
The light banished from the sky behind,
An industrial sunset oiling the sea.
I watch them emerge from the last wave,
Young men and girls grinning like dolphins
In their rubbers, surf-riders swept
Suddenly onto this table of dark sand
And thrift, the coastline's low moraine.

And back again to the conflict with water,
Wiping salt-stiffened hair from their eyes,
The flimsy boards pitching like driftwood
On the swell, flattening with the ebb.
Theirs, briefly, is a perilous excitement
When the current lifts them high
And they stand erect on roofs of water,
Balanced on the summit of a wave.

And there they glide, untouchable,
The moment of flight and their bodies'
Instinctive mastery lasting until
They are somersaulted into the foam
And they creep to shore exhausted,
Barefoot, wincing with the discriminate
Steps of thieves, aware perhaps
Of something they might have won, or stolen.

Dock

Greek and Irish, the shy Somalian
Make common language the city's nasal whine;
Brothers on the wharf as the cargoes
Come swinging overhead: oranges,
Iron, feldspar, grain, out of the sky
The world's tangible gift, a pittance now
As a shadow shift works the freighters,
Alexandra Dock reproachful with echoes
And this south part of the city an empty hold.

In the chart shop maps like dust sheets hang
From drawing boards, and a last technician
Traces blue fathom lines, as delicate
As webs, the irregular shelving
Of a coast eight thousand miles away.
His pen unlocks the sea. It roars in my head.
The compasses stride a continent
From the white edge of its desert coast
To the equatorial heart; a vessel
Manoeuvres into green Bahia,
Its cabins a dizzying fug of languages.

Walking the dock I find that world
Has vanished like a ship's brief wake.
Across the road the seaman's mission
Is a sour honeycomb of rooms,
The walls of dormitories marbled by the damp.
But where the money came ashore
The banks are moored, ornate as galleons,
All dark Victorian mortar
And the sudden frosts of engraved glass,
Their sooted corbels thrusting like
The jaws of Exchange millionaires.
Straight down to the water's edge
The road runs like a keel.

Snaps

After the rain the small rockpools
Glitter like a switchboard.
The girls wait by the photobooth
Until the card of snaps slides down the shute.
Impossible, they clutch themselves
And stagger, hurt with laughter
In a wild circle. All strangers these,
For whose face matches the idea of self,
That coveted identity, closed like a locket,
The first secret? They've snarled and pouted,
Hid themselves behind the mask of the absurd.
The images come glossy, wet,
Like something born.

'The Kingdom of Evil'

Afraid of the dark, of being alone,
We come here to investigate
The cause of our unease, the root of a fear
That's a common bond; our inheritance.

Heads torn from bodies, limbs with the pale
Glimmer of fungi; and under glass
A simple and ingenious device
For causing as much possible pain

To a human being. The technology
Is plausible but the terror lies elsewhere.
Here are young men with pushchairs, their giggling
Teenaged wives in wild mascara, tight denim,

And the imperturbable middle-aged
Looking in different directions.
The commentary has a neutral tone,
The history of torture like the history of art,

Periods, schools, the great virtuosi
Of the craft. The henbane Doctor Crippen used
Is a quiver of plastic leaves,
The Yorkshire Ripper wears a tuxedo.

At the exit sunlight slaps the face
And all the smirking children wander off
Into the fair. Behind us, in a darkened room,
The tracery of wax restores
A gleaming tear, the psychopathic grin.

The Attic

The ceiling shows the yellow stains
Where snow blew into the attic,
A paper-thin pale moss upon the beams
Wetting my hands as I swing
My weight in through the trap-door.

That frontier crossed, I take to trespassing.
The attic room a pelt of dark, the house's
Dreamless skull. I pause and listen,
Crouched sprinter-like over the boards.
And slowly there identify
The architecture of the drifts,
Their frozen combs of snow a yard high.

The torchbeam's dirty stripe of light
Lies brutal as a scar; no snow falls,
For these pillars have erupted
Like fungi, the midden in the middle
Of the floor a sheet draped on a chair.

In the room below my daughter fights
With sleep, her breath a handsaw's icy rasp;
Above, the aerial's hollow stem
Scraping its bracket. Panic has a metal taste.
Everywhere the mercury-coloured pools
Of settling snow lap against the joists,
And here beneath a broken slate
A drift of lilies grows taller by pale atoms.

I cannot touch this profligate:
The snow is furtive and obscene,
And when the wind rises the attic fills
With particles of light, a television
Screen that sucks me in. The blizzard
Is in the house, its voice like pigeons,
Such soft insistence on its mastery.

And I find I have always lived elsewhere,
That I have never known this place:
Old clothes and broken furniture, a bath
Of bulbs with tendrils black as candlewicks,
Sparkless but for snow. I breathe and hear
A breath returned, the flutter as
My daughter's voice thaws and freezes,
Freezes, thaws, and streetlight falls
Out of the roof like flakes of orange rust.

The drifts are grey and tiered like hives,
The swarming snowpoints hover and subside.
Ice on my clothes is fine as insect-wings.

from *Breaking Down*

A leaping boy with pollen-coloured hair,
That girl whose creaky leg-iron
Looked like the letter H. The teeming past,
Enigma of memory! Your childhood
Was the story I never quite believed,
Its hoard of detail challenging
The present's sparser life.
But thrilling, such talent for swift recall,
The lacquered moments from history's fog.
A children's council meets again
In a clearing of a wood, yellow grass
And the cool baize of moss, a circle
Of foxgloves, tall, wizard-like,
And lichen black as surgical stitch
A sharp seam on the rock. So the dead,
The sick, the mad, the amnesiac,
Those for whom the past has been
The cruellest of times, ally once more
In youth's confederacy; before
They vanish, ghosts in frayed jerseys,
Faces stained with the dust of moths
And dandelion milk. Leaving time on your hands.
Now the hours shoot away
Like seeds from the broom's black pods;
Each day a small, dry detonation,
And the fruit gone.

*

In this city a reek of malt
The characteristic pungency.
City of breweries and their
Seaweed rankness, the waste
Poured down the river's sluice
In a floe of yellow foam.

69

District of locked Victorian
Streets silent behind zinc:
Spice baskets green with dill,
Orange with turmeric:
Mr Arakan never closes till ten;
His posters fly, slashing like gullwings.

Tenement of olive brick,
A dormitory with bare plumbing.
The ledges of that bed have known
A hundred like you set to trace
The lost property of their lives.
But eyes squeezed shut can't black us out.

*

They walk and cup the precious cigarettes,
Pace the corridors and sun-flooded ward,
Smoking, stubbing, relighting the butts,
Look comic, vacant, desperate and bored.

I want to give him a lovebite, the red-
Head says, eyes polished like bits of quartz;
In my arms tonight not in my thoughts,
I want to have him lying in my bed.

On the ceiling the black stalactite
Of someone's meal, the deep tan of the smoke
An older stain. Out of here in a week
If I wanted, they say; I could come tonight,

Pack a suitcase and walk over the hill,
Feel the frost sting like a hypodermic,
Hear the river running when the air is still.
Or less than a week: perhaps less than a week.

I want to take my man to the ward, that's all,
I want to kiss his mouth until it hurts,
Or less than a week, past the cattle
Grazing in Cae Morfa, breath pouring like spurts

Of milk. I know, I've pulled their tits,
Their eyelashes like beautiful moss, so womanly,
His body next to mine a few minutes,
So silent, patient, a hot side touching me.

*

You threw the tablets in the toilet bowl:
Orange, red and black their slow suspensions
In water, like the fruit clusters
Of the wayfaring tree, its bitter lozenges.

The whole house is a medicine-cabinet.
About the rooms the bottles lie with tops
You cannot unscrew, barbiturates
Like bryony's grapes, and the small
Metallic rattle of some forgotten dose
Seeds in a pod. Their coloured grains
Are pollen that escapes a cracked capsule.

We hang stones on your limbs, parch your lips,
Tie you to a chair and drain the well
Of your mind, fill your mouth with ashes
And your body with dead flowers,
Thrust the scissors' steel against the stems of your hair.

There's a cloud in your eye but no protest.
Every step is now
A particular greeting of the dust. Such care.
And words, being migratory,
Have all gone.
These pills work.

*

We would go there for fossils, the cliffsides
Rich with those shadows of life, ammonites
Curled tight as catherine-wheels, the grey bodies
Of rockpool creatures chalk-marks on a slate.
Our chisels freed them from the steep limestone.

Now a taxi takes you to that quiet place
Through a resort still off-season; a child
Plays in a farm beili, dun farrow and
A green silo the afternoon's landmarks.
Such things might stop the heart, or mean nothing.

The weather clear, but you in overcoat
And boots; there's still a sinew in the wind
And surf is booming at the mouths of caves,
The moraines of coloured plastics on the shore
And all the bleached hillocks of sea-litter.

'A good day for a walk', he says, 'have fun',
And spins the red Cortina through the lanes.
And then there is only you and the great
Game of forgetting, an act of concentration
Meant to dissolve a life. Like blowing a sparrow's

Egg perhaps, dark, still, and rough as ice
That perfect thing, a scribble on its shell.
So you move against the slow current
And your calves ache as the next wave slaps
Like some cold green fern over your coat,

And then you are in the undergrowth
As the water opens around you huge
Colourless flowers with a choking scent,
A noose of vines that plucks you from your feet.
Soon the roots of the forest are pressed against your mouth.

Tight as an ammonite you lie curled
In the white stone of the bed. A face of chalk,
And salt-stiff hair that brushes can't untie,
Arranged upon your sheet. Do fossils dream?
Tomorrow when you wake we'll talk and talk.

from

The Looters

(1989)

The Looters

The helicopter cameras
Bring us the freeze frames.
A black sea outlines each peninsula
As snow finer than marble dust
Blurs the steeples of the spruce.
Bad weather, the wisdom goes,
Brings a community together.
Tonight the screen is a mirror
And the news is us.

At a house in Bedlinog
A drift has left its stain
Like a river in flood
Against the highest eaves.
There will be a plaque placed there soon
As if for some famous son,
While the cataract at Cwm Nash
Is a thirty foot long stalactite
Full of eyes and mouths
And the dazzling short circuits
Of a pillar of mercury.
An icicle uncirclable by three men.

Abandoned on the motorway
The container lorries are dislocated
Vertebrae. The freeze has broken
The back of our commerce
While on the farms, the snow-sieged
Estates, people return
To old technologies.

Meat is hung in double rows,
The carcasses identified
By the slashing beams.
Each one looms hugely,
Puzzling as a chrysalis
Under its silver condom of frost.
They sway like garments on a rack

When padlocks break and the freezer-
Doors swing out. It is too cold
Here to trail blood, where bread
Is frozen into breeze-blocks
And ten thousand tubes of lager
Sparkle under their ripping caul.
As flashlights zigzag up the wall
Tights turn red and tropical bronze
In each thin wallet.

The stranded drivers sleep in schools,
Their groups determined to uphold
The constitution of the snow.
Families smile through thermos-steam,
A child with her kitten, blue
As a cinder, sucking a blanket:
The usual cast of winter's news
As the commentary runs its snowplough
Through the annihilating white.

Outside, the cars are scoops
Of cumulus, and toboggans
Polish gutters in the drifts.
We never see the looters.
They move somewhere in the darkness
Through the blizzard, beyond the thin
Bright crescent of the screen,
Those people who have understood the weather
And make tomorrow's news.

Yops

It waits for them
In the shadow, the rainsmoke.
The pines' blue quills
Sweep over it, and roof pitch
Blinks with all its lizards' eyes.
Then daylight turns its huge key
In the lock.

The shed fills up with fizzing smells and words.

The tabletop's burnt with their names
For each other, the scorched identities
Of this year's clutch of teenaged working men

Kicking the clodges round
In parched boots bracketed with lime
And studs like quillets, their brutal jewellery.
Through denim shreds move the cartoons
Of last year's loves and hates.

Over picks and mattocks
They push inside.
Over green cement dust frozen into ribs across the floor
They warm themselves on language hot as rum.

Wait an hour.
Feel the moods erupt, dissolve. Twitching
Like lurchers they face a world framed by a door
And walls where girls are starfish,
Sulky eels.

Low as rainsmoke, thermos-steam
The great frustrations hang.
Steelies start to tap the leaking boards.

Ants

(For Australia in 1988, on its 'Bicentennial')

In the bar you watched the miners
Try to drink the uranium
Out of their bellies, each frayed
Green page of the bankroll
Waved like a new discovery.

Behind the backdoor in the yard
Are the grey-haired men and women
Rubbing their misshapen dugs,
The still uncertain tight-browed boys
Finally tearing the ringpulls

From the fizzing cans, spilling
Oblivion over the grass
As a tribe of worker-ants appear
And roll the sweetened crumbs of earth
Back to their pavilions.

Perhaps it was your skin, the colour
Of their bootsoles, those men didn't like.
But they too are as dark as the cliff's
Obsidian the company's
Impatient dynamite reveals.

What they could not understand
Was not being able to ticket you
With one of the street's natural
Felonies, those predictably
Contagious lusts

That fill one side in the notebook,
Especially when the sand, storm-whipped,
Rattles the beerhouse walls
And spins in a ragged helix
About the edge of town,

Its grains swarming
Around the neon bulbs
Like ants on desert orchids.
But your behaviour they could tell
Was no bad weather incivility.

Your people once walked
Down the spine of a continent,
Discovering the one right name
For the lizard, the right name for the tree,
Laying the highway with their songs.

Now your father swats at daylight
In his corral of cans,
Sometimes pushing a broom for a dollar
Around the trailer-park.
He is the chief who serves at the diesel-pump,

Magician without a memory,
Watching and offering no comment
As the young men suck the whisky stem,
Then pour gasoline
Over the ant-thrones. In the dark

They whisper like phosphorus,
Those beacons that once had names,
The hot, red kilns where a people
Unmakes itself. Vivid as a cave-
Painting, each gallery turns to flame.

The meagre room they put you in
Has a bucket and a striped pillow,
The graffiti-scrawl of insect-blood.
You're drunk on words, the gaoler says,
That newspaper talk about rights.

At dawn the men in yellow trucks
Burrow across their mooncrater,
A hole to lose this township in.
Around the shacks your dogs still sleep,
And if there's an absence

No one speaks of a drinking-place unfilled
Or a gap in the welfare line.
So many of your sort might not appear
For days or weeks before the slow
Perplexed acknowledgement of wrong.

That there was trouble in the night
Is murmured and shrugged off:
There's no one with the name for it,
The one right word that measures you
Hung by your shirt-sleeve in the cell

Like a sheaf of drying flowers,
A few spilled petals on the floor below.
They've murdered language, killed the one
Whose speech might act as searchlight through
The coagulating dark,

And name the action, name the act.
It's a big country with spaces on the map
And so many things to fill it with,
While the ants are placing grain on grain
In the circles of white ash.

Development Area

The chimneys work all shifts,
Flying their pennants of flame.
And where technicians crash
A ball about, the corals
Are a jumbled alphabet
In the tar.

At Crymlyn the prehistoric
Debris works out of the soil
Its monument to amnesia:
Plastics and metal and fine
Blue polythene
Like the wrappings of a city.

It's a territory of sirens;
But step behind the lorry park
And sulphur falls with the dew,
While down the glossy bark
Of the birches runs lichen
Like a lipsticked kiss.

Offices are hourglasses,
Secretaries their grains of sand.
On the glacier of the city's
Rubbish the children pick
For futures already discarded.
There is light here, but no window.

Sunglasses

*(On the visit of Mrs Margaret Thatcher
to Porthcawl, 21 June 1986)*

We come to watch and to wait:
Perhaps to shout. Twenty people
On the promenade, an arc of the sea
Behind us, and a police dog in streaming
Gold fording a rock pool.

At my shoulder a small pressure:
A man in a grey suit
And sunglasses, his red crewcut
Like a saucer of iron filings.

Above us the legs of the police
Are screwed into stone;
Strangers on the roofs squint
Through lenses, their cameras
Feeding on our shadows.

And suddenly our chorus is blowing away.
I can examine my voice
As if it was a creature washed from the sea.
Then someone waves and the black
Limousines have disappeared.

In the restaurant we queue for takeaways.
Hello, says a voice. You're finished now?
The aluminium foil
Is like a mirror in his hands,
A bead of sweat on every thorn of his hair.
Then he puts on his sunglasses
And rubs out my face.

The Mansion

The house stands as it always has,
Its windows tall above the lake
And grass cut almost to the yellow root.

Along the drive a whitelimed kerb
Follows a perfect crescent,
As if stone, like air or water, moved in waves.

My steps dissolve in gardens where
The acid rhododendron thrives,
Its flowers pink and white as naked dolls.

It always was a selfish tree,
Devouring the light, growing
Glossy and alone, the strong inheritor.

At the door they take my card
And a name in silver italics
Grants entry where I never thought to pass.

These hands laid gently on my arm
Disturb an earlier trespasser,
That child under the yew hedge

Who watched the long cars slide through his village
And women shaped like candleflames
Moving over the lawns.

Above his head the berries swelled
As soft as wax around each nucleus,
The black nugget of poison that would grow.

The Verger

Every day his bonfire
The shape of a tepee
Showed its reluctant smoke.

Springs through a mattress those thin coils,
The cut grass glowing like tobacco
As he fanned it with a sack.

Later I'd walk over to where
A thrush had smashed a tigerstriped snailshell
And the wires of a wreath

Lay like a burnt-out catherine-wheel.
Brambles covered the graves,
A ball of caterpillars pulsed in its silk nebula,

And there on the fire would lie
The bodies of snakes the verger had hunted
Through the cool, vitreous ivy of the hedge,

The harmless grass-adders he'd swung like flails
Against a piece of marble coping
In that vendetta he pursued

Daily and determinedly
Against the graveyard's secret life.
Perhaps he thought it exposed some mystery,

Leaving the grass-snakes there
With damp-scorched testaments
And dead hydrangea heads like dolls' wild hair.

Agate green and grey
Ran the traceries of grass-snake skin,
Their scissor-jaws agape.

Slowly the bonfire toppled
Like an angel into the weeds.

from *Fairground Music*

NUNS BATHING

From the garden to the dunes
Laughter threads their single file.

Brown as fieldfares
They move towards the waves

And climb the sea-eaten wall
For the green pencils of samphire,

Smiling at something not of this place
And sniffing their lemony fingers.

Each one holds a camera.
Their children are already conceived.

DOUBLE ENGLISH

When the inspector walked into the room
Mr Holt's eyes grew cloudy as lemonjuice.
He was giving out a poem by Walter de la Mare,
Still sooty from the photocopier
And warm in the hand.

Mr Holt taught in a girls' school
Because he liked boys.
Years ago in another place
He had taken two lads to the funfair
And they had all travelled upside down
On the Wheel of Fate.
The money had fallen out of Mr Holt's pockets,
But it was better than double English.

The inspector took a copy to the back seat.
He was a headquarters-type of person
In nescafé-coloured trousers.
Politeness left a cool space around him.
It was only a short poem,
And Mr Holt had found it in a very old book,
The one he always used for poetry lessons.

The ghost-train was hot and stuffy
As a wardrobe. A green face
Shone in the darkness like a luminous clock.
Mr Holt put his hand on the knee
Of one of the boys. He put out his hand
And there was screaming and laughter
And the echoes of laughter.
Then the doors banged open
And his headmaster was standing by the ticket-booth.

Reading the poem, Mr Holt listened to the echoes.
There were words in it
You never heard any more
And things that might be difficult to explain.
Mr Holt had never been much good at explanations.
The page was cold.
And glancing at the clock of the inspector's face
He noted there were exactly fifty-eight minutes to go.

GHOST TRAIN

A paperback novel
Placed cover up,
The headphones pulled down tight
Inside her hair.

No need to talk.
She pushes out tickets with the change
And we step into a carriage
On the rail.

Through the cracks in their fingers
Our children
Squint at oblivion.
The soundtrack's running down like a lit fuse.

And from her hutch of glass
This girl stares out,
The disc of tickets turning on its spike.
Her purple nails
Are filed like arrowheads.

BRONZE AGE

Fat and black
As a fern shaft's sickle root
It lies where I turned
Over that zinc sheet
I will never inch back into place.

Like these helleborines
Snake-lipped and -eyed,
Gleaming with nectar,
It fixes the gaze
With an old narcotic.

In the wreck of the dunes
It basks amongst tokens
Of all our squalid summers;
Its abandoned sleeve of skin
A broken spiderweb.

Only the voltage of fear
Keeps the current
Running between us.
And then I understand:
Through this litter-dappled park

The Bronze Age
Has sent an emissary:
Smudged ace of diamonds
On its neck, the hollow tooth
A tiny phial of delirium.

IN THE ARCADE

The money hangs over a precipice:
One nudge and it should fall.
Strange it never works like that
And soon the slots are jammed
And a man unlocking the sump of coins.

Forced to his knees he embraces it,
The silver, slippery money-child
That has leapt into his arms.
At their machines the gamblers pause,
Then look away from a private act.

MADAM ZEENA

A breeze moves the plastic
Skirts of the hut
As she traces the palm's hieroglyphic.

Under the curtain
The feet of a fast-food queue,
The dabs of paint and effervescent rusts
On the Wheel of Fate.

And at her table
A fat schoolboy, nodding
And pink-freckled as an orchid,
Cheekbones rouged by sunlight
In the chalk of his face;

A lunchtime schoolboy
Awkward and shivering in the gloom,
As the mystery of what happens
Is confessed to him.

FATHERS

Flat out amongst the towels
And empty flasks they lie
As their fathers might have done,
Eyes closed, not sleeping,
But for a time untouchable,
As if a line was drawn
Around them in the sand.

Their children play on a mat
Of restharrow, crinkly as a perm,
The radio's tuned to the tumult
Of contemporary lusts.
Along their shoulders' thickening yoke
Tattoos fade to a mockery
Of everything they thought they could predict.

Isolation Ward

The hypodermic is big
As a bicycle pump.
She slips the blade
Between blue vertebrae
And I count in a language
I have never learned
Until it is released.

I grow thin and polished
As the rim of a wheel,
Squeezing the delirious
Animals out of my mind
To make the audience gasp –
Sad relatives erect
In their uniforms of flowers.

No one touches me but her
Whose duty is each day
To take the hot stones from my head
And stroke me with the irises
Picked on the moor, transparent
Webs of ice the last petals,
Green bottles of a dangerous seed.

Then she whispers far into my sleep
Teaching me to walk.
My cheek's upon the silver
Eye of her watch, face clenched
In her groin. Behind glass
The children are like thistledown
She is blowing towards home.

In the Watchtower

The frontier hums, a live
Cable carrying our charge.
Barbed wire and the sentry posts
Bristle against a wall of acid firs:
Climbing the steps I'm brushing off
Their needles hooked into my clothes,
The needle wax's scent of oranges.

It's safe here in the clock-tower –
The villagers' dovecote –
Where sunlight varnishes the boards
And soldiers lean their guns
Against a wall, put down
Binoculars and take to twisting round,
Like farmers with a barren hen,
The necks of tall bottles.

And I smile as they step, dainty as girls,
Out of the rifles' harnesses,
Thinking of my grandfather
And the scornful way he'd leave his spade
After a morning's couch-cutting,
Relief flexing through the racked
Sinews, yellower than iris roots,
And spreading from the halfmoons of his sweat.

I've never seen a gun so close,
This grey snub-barrelled thing
Shining like a beetle's carapace,
No bigger than a toy's image.
But touching it might set the bells
Above us, now a cluster of blue grapes,
Speaking the first syllables
Of the last war, and loose the doves –
Preening on the shoulders of bellmetal –
In a volley over Czechoslovakia.

Those fields swim in a blue-green haze
Like the pages of a passport.
I stop, and feel the current stir
Beneath me, two armies praying
To the eager god of electricity,
While a family of leverets
Wild as pinball in the grass
Cross frontiers within sight but out of range.

A Footnote to the History of Bridgend

In a cellar up the lane
The future is about to happen.
A boy opens his fist
And the mauve tablet lies there
Like a pinch on his skin.
He grows as pale as elderwood.

Guitars come out of the vans
And all the unrecognisable
Schoolgirls line themselves against
The walls, a different insignia
At their throats, eyes sooty
As the shy, tree-hurdling lemur's.

They hug each branch of chill
Brickwork as Pink Floyd stir
The cauldron. I am on the hill
Behind the yellow eldertrees
Watching the birth of 1966.
This might be anywhere, say the cynics;

The fact that it is not
Will only occur to me
When it is too late, ours never being
A precocious country.
Meanwhile in the nextdoor barber's shop
Instruments tremble on glass shelves.

The Hot-House

1

Madness:
To be utterly
Without humour.

I watch obsession
Narrowing the grey
Meniscus of your eye.

This year the first you do not note
That hour of frosty spring
When the oak spurns its leaves

And they lie
Like brickred pheasant down
After a kill.

2

Evenings were spent around the hearth
Examining the anthology of flames.

See what you will in the orange
Honeycomb the coals become,

Every year the yuckers still fall
Down the spiral of the smoke,

Starlings tipped from the nest's wild raft
To catch a moment on the hooks of flame,

Their throats' yellow triangles
Part of the fire, opened as if for food,

Before flesh becomes bracken,
The skeletons of leaves,

The ghosts of flowers
In your abandoned books.

3

Today we walk in the rainforest
Under its hangar of glass.

There is a device there now,
An electric clock whose numbers

Spin remorselessly. Time is
Burning backwards towards zero

As the forest shrinks in front of us,
An acre destroyed every second.

This leaflet in my hand
Might be all our biographies.

It tells of species that become extinct
Before they are discovered.

4

Padlocks snap on the harvest,
Small flames run relays
Down the stubble lines.
This afternoon is hot and moist
As a coin held in the fist.

At three o'clock the curtains
Drawn, the electric fire's
Single bar a humming
Artery inside the room.
The t.v. whispers its conspiracies.

You stir the sugar through
Your tea but hardly touch its sweet
Mortar, as one by one
The noises of the street
Send you erect and shivering to the glass.

There's no one there.
There never is. Only the roses
Tapping with their thorns the other
Side of the pane, and my own voice
Stirring, stirred

To nothing in the unbearable room.
Then I touch your dress
And all its electricity
Meets me like a blow.
Your sweat's the frosty scum of exhaustion.

There's nothing that can warm
You here. I've never felt
A skin so cold, a grip so tight.
And I leave you now
Spinning like a petal in a web.

5

In this part of the forest
All the creatures are unique.

Here is a woman
With nine rings on her fingers
And wine a garnet in her cup.

96

Her voice is like a tape
Played backwards, her mouth becoming
A black spool of words.

She points about her through the ward
At the jaguar's sulphuric
Eye, the webs of rain
That shiver in the treeferns.

We want to destroy them
Before we have understood.
It's fear of their strangeness
That lifts the weapons in our hands.

6

We come down from the upstairs ward
On the fire-escape's spiral.
Wolf-spiders hang their scaffolding
About us like a mist,
The wasps corkscrew
Through troughs of fallen fruit.

Behind the wall the garden has
Recovered its freedom.
Only us today on a morning walk
And a gang of boys beneath the chestnut trees,
White legs flashing through nettles
And the nettles' yellow stems

Hollow as hypodermics,
Splintering underfoot.
I think of the apples by your bed,
Their pale green pyramid untouched:
This year is turning profligate,
Its elderberries faded

To dull newsprint, the chestnuts
Only milky embryos
The boys have burst too soon.
Something I have to say, you said,
And I wait for the words that don't exist
That will pick this lock of grief.

Halfway down the tall staircase,
Its iron hoops like dinosaur bones,
You look around as if surprised
To see how far we've come.
There's a step towards me and a step away:
You're waiting there to choose.

7

Mornings and evenings
The same nurse lets us in.
He's worked a week of doublers,
Earning the authority
Of exhaustion, that mauve
Rim of the eye, the slight
Amused detachment
Of someone who has stopped
Testing himself. He brings
A hoop of keys, big as a wreathwire,
From the television lounge.
After seventy-eight hours
He is letting you go.

8

When you come for the weekend
You bring eighteen pairs of shoes,

And speak, it is a proverb,
Of the green damsons behind the wall,

A tree's bitter pebbles
That a week later will be

Mauve-skinned nipples
Squeezed and rolled around the mouth.

Now the miraculous tablet
Clings to your tongue,

You take communion
Four times a day.

The white crystal dissolves
And its dust lightens your eye

As one poison meets another
And sets you moving again

Through the first day, the second,
A week. A phial of pills

Stands on the shelf; lighter than eggshell,
Bitter as green damsons.

9

Under glass the air grown succulent
With heat. Above us the belfries
Of hibiscus and palm, a dead
Dateleaf like wet cardboard.
From the trees' silkscreen
The colours cloud and run.

We hold our coats,
Perspire, and gaze around.
Here's a bush that stands its flowers as
A collection of fine porcelain,
A kind of moss with blooms like Saturn's rings.
The arrows point through steamy latitudes.

But no tropical switchboard
Of voices here. Only temperate lives
Confused by the architecture of the plants,
Stunning grotesques whose petals lie
Like gobs of paint, whose stems
Are freakish torsos, dark and oiled.

You trail your bag with other visitors.
There's no way into the dangerous feast.
The sexless bees rave in the air
Or force an entry at a dragon's throat.
We watch each gleaming sphincter
Squeezing shut.

Behind this glass
The city's clocks,
The looks of those who might have
Ventured in, but would not
Change their stride.
So you make your way

Down the aisles of the rainforest,
Its colours erupting
Out of the dark green patina
Of night, lost for now
In something stranger than yourself.
Like the undiscovered peoples of the world.

from
Hey Fatman
(1994)

Archaeology

He lies where
He buried himself,

Bones laid out like a toolset,
Ratchets, broken levers,
All smeared the colour of starlight.

He swam, he flew,
He kicked the moon's dust
Into a typhoon;

Stole a piece of the sun
And burned himself,

Sent the tides backwards
And made the rivers flow uphill.

They say he ran shouting
From his house with his hair on fire,

A madman
Who forgot his own name.

Harriet

There were Christmas cards and cups of tea
But after an hour of the class
I knew I was losing them.

Six faces, December-pale, had begun
To glance outside at a day
That had never really started.

The sky was like the cratered asphalt yard
Where the caretaker now laboured
With a delivery of smokeless fuel.

'Why don't we try something new?'
She whispered, the almost pretty one,
The one with a gold tooth and a physics degree.

Odd, but everyone seemed to know
At once exactly what she meant.
They brought a glass from the kitchen,

Cut a crude paper alphabet,
Then dragged the desks together for our board.
And there was my finger on the glass,

Touching, as if feeling for a pulse,
My dry forefinger, beckoning,
On the tumbler's thick green hull.

O spirits, I thought, in whom I do not
Yet believe, how we must bore you
With this inquisition. And why, O phantoms,

Should you bother with our words?
But the glass grew warm and slowly
Began to tremble on the board.

'You see,' said a blue-haired grandmother,
Eerily matter-of-fact, 'we have called a presence down
And it must do as we bid.'

Our time was up. We should have left it there.
But the graduate was not content.
She asked our visitor to name itself,

And this time the glass shimmied like mercury,
Then seemed to float above the desk,
Surely unimpelled by our light touch.

I saw the science die in both her eyes,
The powder on her face stand up, erect
As frost. And she was out across the yard,

Her Metro gunned towards the town
Before we understood the spelled out word:
H·A·R·R·I·E·T: the name of her dead child.
The envelopes lay ripped beside her chair.

The Swift

The hall is cold, the stairwell dark,
And in my hand the brandy glass
Warm as a child's brow.
I answer the eleventh ring
And hear my question, furred with wine,
Its tiny echo fading like
A lightbulb's filament.

This is the sound the radio makes
When the anthem is played at midnight
And then engulfed by the inaudible
Electric breath between stars.
There's no one there, no human voice
Describing why it telephones
At this desperate hour for telephones.

But I sit with my hot disc
Of liquor and listen to the fever
Of static, the racing brain-code
Of it that listens to me, and notices
The quickening pulse in my temple
Where the telephone is pressed,
The prickling of my hair.

And I overhear my car outside
Cooling like the brush of moths
Against a shade. This is the voice
Of dust that settles on its empire,
The sound that left my hand tonight
When I picked the swift,
Like a fallen evening-glove,

Dying from the road,
And spread its black crescent
Upon my palm. The weight of a glass.
But now the air tightens
To a strait-jacket around the heart,
And three words like maroons explode
Hard inside the ear.

Are
They ask. And hugely wait.
You
– A Saharan interval.
Happy?
And there's a desert in that voice
Come to me from the end of the world.
Now the brandy's hot as a test-tube,
Its perfume clotting in my throat,
And slapping the wall this hand can't find the switch.

Daisy at the Court

'Arithmetic and manners, start with those':
And he had left her on the stair
And gone off after partridges, small bundles
Of feathers you'd tread on before they'd move.

So this was it. A house as long as a street,
Stone lions, and the Welsh language
In a shield on the portico. One of the children
Already pawed the darkness under her skirt.

In a newspaper once she had wondered
At the Cherokee leader who claimed
The worst part of exile was having nowhere
To bury your dead. 'Yes,' she murmured,

Picturing homesickness as a white
Lily, one of those flowers grown
For the graveside, a field of lilies
Whose perfume was a secret shared only by herself.

'This isn't home,' breathed the nanny, a girl
Whom no child had sucked, thinking of
The charcoal ovens in Dean, no bigger
Than beehives, the warmer vowels:

This was foreign, even the bread was strange,
And at dinner the men came out
Of the greenhouses and looked at you when
Your back was turned. Especially the ones with wives.

And yet. There was Ivor, most often Ive,
(Christian names in this country split in half)
Who saluted every morning, except once,
When his hands were cupped for her in a nest

Of blond apricots; who had walked her down
To a corner of the long garden,
Where water was spun across terraces,
Looped and stretched over rocks, before falling

Like a roll of silk into a pool.
'This is a palace,' he had said. 'At Catterick
We slept fifty to the barrack-room
And still the windows froze on the inside:

'In the village we cut the avenue
Of elms, a hundred years old, for firewood;
There's some eat only gooseberries and milk.
But here is a place hard times don't touch.'

She had looked at him then and felt
All the ghostly answers of a sum unwritten,
As the Wolseley bit into the drive's gravel
And a man leaped out and strode towards her.

from *A History of Dunraven*

THE ICE TOWER

They packed it in straw,
Carried it on paddles to the kitchen,
Were grateful for its constancy.

And in its cellar
Ice comforted itself,
Fed like grief upon its own image.

Ice was master
And mistress in this tower,
Its ridged wall the colour

Of dragonflies, its sweat
Pearling the darkness,
The gutter running as it sloughed

A snakeskin of glacial
Purples, ebb-tide greys.
I listened, said the scullery-maid,

Hurrying down from the castle
One June evening, the gorse
Ecstatic as goldfinches;

And heard the sound it made, a lover's
Groan, something I should not say.
I rushed out to the gate-house

Frightened of a footfall
Not my own. But there was nothing.
Only the tower behind, its door bolted

And my poor hands raw
From where I had sawn the blocks;
No splinters, yet the slow needlework of blood.

Lists mainly, in shaming Latin.
Epitaphs for next year. Next week.

Of course, there are peoples too
Who might be honoured in its pages:

The Kreen-Akore, the Mandans:
Their stone-age pinioned by cameras.

But of the inhabitants of Dunraven
Only one is named, falco peregrinus,

Gwalch glas, peregrine, the slayer
Of racing fowl, fox of the loft.

I saw Enoch Powell once, tiny,
Squat as a goshawk, shaking

With rage as he described a plot
That had done him down.

The crowd was not prepared to blink. It knew
The danger there like a rank smell of its own.

And every June the peregrines
Quarter the cliff; ultimate ferocity

With nowhere to go. Their beaks
Are tin-openers for the sternum,

Clawgrip an iron-maiden lock.
That sort of purity can't last.

Meanwhile, in the Non-Political,
For the second night, three men spread maps

On a table-top, open a jewellery-box
With a satin base, soft as a bean-pod.

Think of the agate that could nestle there;
The garnets. They dint the fine material,

Prepare a place of honour
For two warm, white stones.

THE LAST MAN

Take this pill, they said.
You will see visions.
Alternatively it will destroy
Any visions you already have.

Bylo gets them in the Club
For the price of a round
And crouches now
Shivering over a caib.

Naked but for cut-offs
And his famished work-boots
With their half-moons of steel
He's white as belly-pork.

I'd send him home
But it's fifteen miles
And he has fifty pence in his pocket.
So he trembles here,

Pupils like the pricks
Of hypodermics,
A buzzard's feather
Behind his ear:

No snap, no flask,
Only that irradiating grin
And the name of his daughter –
Arianwen –

Like something his blade has found
Gleaming in the ruin;
A kind of wealth
Making him dangerous.

The Swimming Lesson

'Out of your depth,' the instructor warns,
But a man might drown in a thimble
Is my philosophy. And for a second
I am sublime. Weightless in a cradle.

'Deep breaths,' she shouts, and now I taste
Blood and oysters as the sea swallows
Me, its invincible salt rubbed in
As I thrash in the shallows.

'Breathe,' she says, 'you need to breathe';
But my body is drawn
Taut as a broom-pod before it detonates.
So this is what it feels like to be born,

I think, before the luxury of breath,
To stammer on the brink of real speech.
And face down in the sand I count
The lipsticked Marlboros that paint the beach

Like sea-rocket, the international
Brand-names discarded by the tide.
This is how I learn to save my life,
To doggy-paddle, porpoise-glide

Into the nameless spaces on the map –
Eryngo-blue isthmus, canal
Of starving eels. But lesson over
I still hold to something more predictable.

'Ah, it's not my element,' was what
I always said, a poor excuse
From one who read no horoscopes,
But not unwise. I knew what might douse

The sun. And so for thirty years
I side-stepped with a genius
All attempts to make me swim.
School was worst. At the local baths,

Brutalised by chlorine and the guards'
Insolent musculature
I would sit in tropic changing rooms
Clutching a forged letter,

Whilst next-door the baffling shouts of joy
Drowned the mutter of the pipes.
Even the nunks and fatties swam,
The twitching academic types

Excused from outdoor sports, a ridiculous
Stick-insect in borrowed costume
Braved the deep-end's fathom and a half.
I watched the clock, immersed in shame.

Water, of course was not to blame.
I happily trawled the tannin-
Coloured streams for dragonflies'
Barbarous larvae, the sharp sewin

And minnows thin as pine-needles,
Always an inch beyond a fingertip.
Waist-deep in that cold current
I'd not trouble how a simple slip

Could dunk this non-swimmer
– Hydrophobic with a bucket of young trout –
Under the Ffornwg's dark plumage of weed,
And keep him there until the light went out.

Somehow, this was different:
A homage paid to a primitive god.
Swimming itself seemed as ludicrous
As flying; quite alien to the blood.

So for thirty years of foolishness
I kept myself to the dry ground.
I never sought that stream again,
The civil war of water and the land.

Now England's the set for a commercial break.
Ten miles out of London, signs warn
Of deer crossing, and here the forest
Is primaeval, soft with lichen

Strung like bladderwrack. Where the trees end
Is the Jolly Fiddler car-park
And Rod Stewart's Lambourghini,
A scarlet flick-knife in the settling dark.

Under the saloon's low eaves
The drinkers watch the pipistrelles
Ricochet off walls of air, hear Essex
Chime with evensong's electric bells.

A traveller here, I still look twice
At machine-guns worn on airport stairs
And a man guarding rare orchids
With chainleashed rottweilers.

But that's England now, and we have stopped
Amidst its eastern breweries
For pizzas from the microwave
And surly pints with yeast thick in the lees.

The mansion here is short-lease flats,
Plasterboard and flaking gloss
Dividing like a honeycomb
The hall and drawing rooms. A Polish

Caretaker waved at the gate-house
As traffic brought home office-
Staff and counter-clerks from Harlow,
Parking beneath a high cornice

Of gargoyles, next to leaded panes.
Bedsitterland in Borsetshire
Was how my friend described the pile,
But I was only eager to explore.

Carp nudged the lake's candelabrum
Of lilies, the vines lay thick
In nettledust. Yet the pool was perfect,
Brimful in a courtyard of glazed brick

With diving-board and spotless changing-room.
Dragged daily by the caretaker
Its oval shone in starlight
Like a polished ballroom floor.

That's how I see it still, a pool
Immaculate under lunar
Continents. I crouched to stroke that silver –
Like the hymen of a coffee-jar –

And felt no old unease.
Adnams' had seen to that of course,
And several shouts of Breakspear's
Chased by unwanted Scotch.

Salacious midnight drew us on
Towards the unlit mansion-house,
Yet the last idea of the day
Seemed one of genius.

Clothes and shoes lay where they fell,
And naked, done with merriment,
I submitted to the shallows' manacles.
Water handles us like a parent,

With a hard, incomprehensible love.
Stiff in its embrace we gasp
For air, choke on impossible
Explanations. Think to escape

And the way we came is covered
By the same rough tide that holds us;
Hate it, and it pulls tighter, our
Nostrils burning with its phosphorus.

There was nothing in the water now
But blackness. I saw my hand on the surface
As if smoothing out the pages
Of some brand-new atlas,

Hesitant strokes to brush away the dark.
The others were invisible,
The sparks of their swimming extinguished
Somewhere at the frontiers of the pool.

A swan, a lily, both are moored
By fury and tenacity
To life. But seeking their mirage of grace
I found instead an icy

Millimetre of pondwater
Beneath my heel. And clearly in that slow
Capsize, I saw the sisters venture
To the beach, laughing, years ago,

To the sea's nunnery, all raw-boned girls
In sheaths of black and glistening plum,
Embracing the first weak wave.
I walked the bay where they had swam –

A knucklebone behind the town –
And heard again their gentle ribaldry,
Saw hair piled high in alice-bands,
Their sealheads all miraculously dry.

Then a fist of water took me in the throat
And an electric bulb shone all
Its hundred watts against my eyes,
The filament a red tongue inside a skull.

Hearing the silence, I think I cried;
If so, the words sank uselessly as iron
Into the pool's still sanctuary.
And there I was a boy again

Bent above a shadow on the stream,
Ragged fringe over the face,
Buttocks pale and thin as willow-leaves:
A hunter in a nameless place.

So thirty years of foolishness
Ended as I dragged my body in,
Spitting the pool's astringency
And moonlight like a nettle on the skin.

Rio Sul

1

She has pitched her booth at the tunnel-mouth.
Here the sun slows us down

Like an American meal,
And we sit on the iron slats

Where the soiled petals of banknotes
Blow around our feet

And each lance of the hibiscus
Shakes its rust over our shoulders.

2

Across this square the candle-seller
Works through the afternoon,

Her bundles of ivory
Built about her like a child's fort.

So many candles today, their flames
Only stone-coloured in daylight,

While the woman stirs chicken-skins
In a sawn-down oil-drum

And her babies lie open-eyed
Like lizards under the stall.

3

Perhaps we have taken someone's seat.
Swimmers come out of the bay,

Towels at their necks like rosaries,
A pavement family sifts our useless change.

But no one claims this place
And under the hoardings beside the church

We sit and watch
A scented metamorphosis,

All the genealogies of wax
Radiant between the yucca leaves.

4

Now here is a candle with a disciple's
Face, considering the square,

A peacock whose blue body
Trails a rick of smoke.

And here is the candle-seller
Under her broken parasol,

Rolling the tallow, trimming the wicks
Black as her children's eyelashes,

The candle-seller heating her stew
On the penitential flame.

Air Lounge Haiku

NEWARK

Latest *Rolling Stone*,
Pitcher of Budweiser.
I think I could live here.

INDIANAPOLIS

Alligator shoes
Speckled with ketchup.
Pottawatomees' holy ground.

O'HARE

Our eyes must surf
One hundred blue screens.
My flight always the next channel.

DENVER

Bourbon round a glacier,
Sodium-free fries.
One mile high and still grounded.

ALBUQUERQUE

Outside, the desert
Like cigarello ash.
Someone will come for you.

SEATTLE

Bag straps manacle
Her wrist. Despite the sirens
Sleep has stolen her.

WASHINGTON

The carousel takes round
A crimson satchel.
Where is the audience?

NEWARK

Luggage outside
Moves like a Raj elephant.
The last ticket is torn.

The Woman from Los Alamos

The snow in the canyon
Has turned grey as driftwood,
Its touch like my grandmother's hand.

Hair of the cactus
Is a sunburn I carry
On my wrist and fingers
As a memory of the cold,

Whilst my shoes disturb
The indian-file of the ants
Marching with their booty
Towards the pyramids.

I had looked down on this country,
The great squares of the states adobe-red,
And seen the fingerprints of glaciers,
The lakes to the horizon scattered
Like the highway's silver hubcaps.

And now here is its soft earth
Holding rocks that refuse to warm,
The nubs of cacti like threadbare tennis-balls,
And an outcropping of quartz
Curious as a meteorite.

The woman from Los Alamos
Stirs the skillet of the soup,
And a thrust with its breast
Full of holes like the snow,
Explores the syllables of alarm.

'Today,' she says, 'the bears came down to the orchard
And forgot to close the gate;
I saw crickets on their yellow wings
Bump-starting in the cottonwoods.

'There are two million acres behind this wall,
Give or take a mountain range,
Full of languages that you will never learn.
Go out and speak in yours.'

Hey Fatman

Me? I was only watching. Nothing else.
It had been one hundred degrees that day
And I'm not used to frying. So I took a seat
Outside and ordered a drink.
The beer came in a glass like a test-tube,
The colour of that monkey, the golden one,
They're trying to save around there,
The one with the mane like a lion.
And Christ, it tasted cold as a dentist's drill.

But after a while I felt the energy
To look around. And I saw
What I expected to see from a street like that:
The last soccer players on the beach,
A big surf pounding, angry, futile
In the place where it always stopped its charge,
And a beggar eating fire,
Walking up and down outside the restaurants,
A magician folding banknotes for his pimp.

At the bar stood the boss in a mildewed tux,
The sweat hanging off him in icicles.
He looked at me once and passed over –
Not important, not a player tonight.
I ordered another to make him doubt,
But he never blinked. You can't buy style.
So I studied his empire's neon sign
Out on the pavement. There was a moth on it
With wings like two South Americas.

It was bigger than my hand. But either
Nobody had seen it or nobody cared.
I wanted to scare it off that scorching globe,
Grab its wings like the old man's black lapels,
But it was impossible to move.
I couldn't get out of my chair,
Couldn't speak. So I sat and looked,
With a radioactive thirst, at the bar
And its imperceptible protocols.

The women were in by now, four of them
At the counter, each holding a drink
With an hibiscus flower in it, and a straw:
One white, one black, two mulatto,
Like my beer. In ones and twos they'd get up
And stroll outside to the pavement,
Amongst the tables, sometimes out of sight,
Wandering around the expense accounts,
As the city's electricity came on.

They weren't collecting for charity,
That's for certain. I couldn't understand
A word, but I knew what their smiles said
As they squeezed past, what their fingernails
Meant as they chimed against glass,
The stick-on ones, red as foxgloves:
Hey fatman, that's what they said;
Almost without saying it, if you know what I mean.
Because that's all it takes in a place like that.

Their earrings said it, their crossed
And uncrossed legs: and off they'd go
With the turks in singlets,
The executives in their button-downs,
Up a darkened stair behind the bar,
And the old man there in opera black
Would smile with his blue iguana lips
As he held the door for them, then pulled it fast,
His armpits dimpled like a garlic-press.

Ten minutes later you'd think there were four
Different girls. No so. The younger ones
Were older now, the brunettes reborn as blondes.
And they'd suck their drinks and circulate,
Trailing a perfume through the room
Of their own sweat, like a herb crushed underfoot.
Hey fatman, it said to the night,
To the brass propellers of the fan
That uttered ceaselessly its quiet scream.

I watched the moth float down like charred paper.
Over the walls the baby roaches ran
Warning of fire, waving their brown arms.
Down through the haloes in my glass
I saw a furnace glow, the table blistering.
A man in the mirror tried to douse his boiling eyes,
But the women of the city combed their hair,
Buckled on silver, strapped on gold,
Then stepped once more out on to its hot coals.